The Rebeats Calfskin Head Book

by Rob Cook

Copyright © 2023, Rob Cook
Rebeats P.O. Box 6, Alma, Michigan 48801
www.Rebeats.com
ISBN: 978-1-888408-58-4

Statue of Jan Žižka by Bohumil Kafka on Vítkov Hill in Prague

Jan Žižka (1360-1424) is a Czech national hero. His military successes became legendary as he repeatedly demonstrated great abilities on the battlefield. He was able to quickly train peasants to successfully challenge better-equipped professional troops and he made the most of emerging technical advances in weaponry.

He lost one eye in battle so he isusually depicted with an eye patch. He eventually lost the other eye as well.

Why is he included in the "skin head" book? It is said that when it became clear that his passing was imminent, he made clear his desire to have his skin tanned and fitted to war drums so that he could continue to inspire his troops and terrify his enemies. It is not clear whether this was actually done.

From a Facebook post by Ryan McKay of Bovid Percussion
"Human skin mounted on human skull caps. 100% the most exotic drum I've ever had the opportunity to work on. A Tibetan Damaru. Seems creepy at first glance, but it's a very significant object in Tibetan Buddhism. Made from the skull caps and scalps of two monks. One of the "heads" had started to separate from the "shell", and I was tasked with getting it back in place. A huge honor. Property of a Buddhist museum in Toronto."

Introduction	1
Amrawco Tips	2-4
Leedy	6-10
Ludwig	11-18
Rogers	19-21
Bovid	22-23
Painted Drum Heads	24-31
More Resources	32
Skin Head Sources	33
Shipping hides (Stern)	34
Links to YouTube Videos	35

Natural Skin Drum Heads- Introduction

Natural hide heads provide a unique playing experience and extremely satisfying feel and sound. They certainly are more expensive than mylar (plastic) heads and require more care and maintenance, but in my opinion are well worth it. There is nothing like the sound and feel of wood on leather.

At one time, there were numerous calf head manufacturers in America. Rogers started out as a tannery and was reknowned at the producer of the highest quality heads available. A number of other drum (and banjo) companies catalogued Rogers heads in addition to their own, with Rogers clearly presented as the premium option. Leedy's heads were also famous, particularly the "UKA" signature series, prepared by the skilled immigrant John Gyuka. Ludwig and Slingerland both operated their own head finishing departments. (For a number of years Ludwig and Slingerland used skins from the same tanneries. Whenever they received word that a new batch of skins were available, both Bud Slingerland and Wm. F. Ludwig II would drop whatever they were doing and race to the tannery in an effort to get first dibs on the finest skins in the new batch.

Eventually all of these companies discontinued their own skin production and purchased them primarily from either Amrawco (American Rawhide Company) or Werco (White Eagle Rawhide Company,) both of Chicago. By the time I became interested in purchasing calf heads in the late 1980s, the only company still producing them in this country was United Rawhide, Mr. Steven Palansky's company in Chicago. Mr. Palansky told me that at one time he sold head to Rogers, Ludwig, Gretsch, and Slingerland. Unable to find a buyer for his business when his health began to fail in the late 1980s, Mr. Palansky prepared to quit business and liquidate. At the eleventh hour he found a buyer, and managed to sell his stock and manufacturing equipment to Stern Tanning which today makes the heads that they sell directly to consumers as well as to resellers such as myself. (They are represented on the Rebeats website as "American" calfskin heads.) These heads represent what I describe as the closest thing to an exact replacement as you can get for most vintage American drums.

There are two tanneries in the British Isles producing high quality heads; one in England and one in Ireland. Both produce wonderful skins which satisfy the most discriminating orchestral percussionists. Neither firm sells their skins tucked (or "lapped") on flesh hoops ready to put on the drum. They are significantly more expensive than the American heads, even before mounting.

There also is a German firm producing high-quality skins.

There are a number of tanneries in Pakistan that are surprisingly easy to do business with. These heads, to date, I've found to be rather low quality. For that reason, I suggest them for use on ceremonial or display drums rather than "players." The problems? Thickness unevenness, color inconsistencies, and tucking problems. When one of these heads has been soaked for tucking, I find that it dries out very quickly and seems to have very little natural glue. By comparison, the Irish heads seem to tuck themselves! (Personally I find this somewhat surprising, considering the Pakistanis are not new to this business. I have in my archives literature which was sent from tanneries in this same province of Pakistan to George Way in 1954.)

Before we discuss the tucking process and the "care and feeding" of calf heads, let's get the terms straight. First there is the drum shell, i.e. the drum itself. The part of the shell that the head rests on is the "bearing edge." The hoop that holds the head on (and is tightened when you turn the tension rods) is the counterhoop. The wooden (sometimes steel) hoop that the skin head is "tucked" or "lapped" on is the flesh hoop. Symphonic guys seem to prefer the steel flesh hoops; they will never twist and mar the finish of a fine instrument. Additionally, they will not warp. I once shipped a calf head mounted on a wood flesh hoop to a customer in another state. When she received it, she called to ask why I had sent such a warped head. I asked her to send it back, and found that the wood hoop had twisted like a pretzel. I phoned Mr. Palansky who informed me that is why he always shipped his heads sealed in plastic; the humidity must be maintained as a constant to prevent warping. I immediately purchased a supply of plastic bags and a thermal sealer. The lesson for my good readers? When you tuck a head, immediately place it on a drum or in a form to "establish the collar", or maintain it's shape.

TIPS ON DRUM HEAD CARE

The following tips are from the booklet "All About Drums" written by John P. Noonan in collaboration with Howard Emery of American Rawhide Mfg Co. and originally published by American Rawhide.

Dampness loosens heads, dryness and heat tightens them; so before playing your drums, adjust them to the tension necessary to counteract climatic conditions.

Use an artgum eraser to clean dry heads. A damp cloth and a little soap will sometimes remove dirty spots.

There are no magic head restoratives. Use only water on heads. Vaseline, oils, or any so-called restoratives only damage them.

When a drum head "roughs up" from wire brushes, sand it very lightly with very fine sandpaper; then wipe with a damp cloth to set nap down.

Drum heads cannot be guaranteed against breakage because they are a product of nature and because much depends upon the way they are used.

There is no set rule as to when a head should be replaced. Much depends on the amount and kind of use it has had. When the snap and response wanes of the head is badly roughed up from wire brushes, get a new head. Don't play on an old worn-out or dead drum head.

Heads should be replaced after several seasons' use— especially tympani heads; for new ones will restore life to your drums.

If you are caught on parade and your drum heads become wet but do not break, mop off all water and allow them to dry slowly. Rain covers will save money. Always carry them on parade.

Patched drum heads never work successfully. If a very small hole or rip appears, tape on both sides with adhesive tape on both sides with adhesive tape to hold until the head can be changed.

Use sticks matched to the head. Don't use "baseball bats" on a small drum or "toothpicks" on a parade drum. Also be sure to have good tympani sticks and bass drum beater.

If the heads of the drums are pulled down too far, retucking is necessary. Soak the heads off the hoops and retuck according to the chapter in this book "How To Tuck Drum Heads."

Always insist on trademarked AMRAWCO drum heads for a genuine quality guarantee. If your music dealer will not supply you with AMRAWCO heads, write us for the name of the dealer in your area who will. DO NOT ACCEPT SUBSTITUTES!

More Amrawco tips
The information here is reprinted from Amrawco's "All About Drum Heads," 1963

Installing New Heads

Remove counter hoop and screws, and take off old heads. Clean edge of shell thoroughly and apply light coating of paraffin around edges of shell. Usually just a slight dampening of the head will be enough so the head will conform to the shape of the drum. Replace hoop and screws and draw head down until it is taut and allow to dry. Then tension to suit. If for any reason the head has warped, sponge thoroughly on both sides until the head becomes soft, which will allow flesh hoop to come back into position. Then place on shell, replace counter hoops and screws, and tension head down about 1/2" all around. Allow to dry thoroughly. If warpage is present, do *not* force the head on the shell, as breakage will probably occur. Sponging the head will allow the flesh hoop to resume a flat position and go on easily. Procedure is the same for batter and snare heads. In placing snare head on the shell, be sure snare bed (depressed surface of hoop) matches snare bed of shell.

Bass Drum

Same Procedure as above. Bass Drum heads are heavier and may require more sponging. All sponging should be done with a clean sponge or cloth, using room temperature water.

Lightly wipe off excess water before head is placed on shell. Be careful that water does not run under flesh hoops when sponging bottom side of heads.

Tympani Heads

When tympani heads are tucked at the factory, they are tucked loosely. However, it is characteristic for tympani to tighten and lose their pocket. It requires time and patience to set a tympani head with the proper collar or pocket. A gradual dampening process repeated every few minutes will slowly slacken the head until there is enough looseness to allow for a collar when the head is pulled down on the kettle. This is accomplished with a damp sponge, wiping the head on both sides being very careful not to get water under or too near the hoop edge. By repeating this sponging every few minutes until the head becomes loose, it does not get too wet all at once and will not discolor. While the head is still damp and loose, pull down to a 3/8-1/2 inch collar, which will allow for a full range of tones.

How To Tension Drum Heads

Since there is no definite pitch factor here, it is difficult to explain the correct playing tension of the snare drum. The drum should be a separate tension (called by some double tension) model, so that the batter head can be drawn a bit tighter than the snare head. The result desired is a crisp, stacatto tone of short duration, with just a little "ring" to give it "projection," or carrying power.

First, test the batter head by placing the forefinger on the center of the head. Press downward a little to determine its tension. If it is about right, the head will depress or "give" a little to slight pressure. If this "give," or depression, is marked, it indicates needed tension.

Starting with one rod, put the drum key in place and give it about a half turn to the right; then go clockwise around (not across) the drum, giving each rod the same amount of turn. Test the tension again until the amount of "give" mentioned above is obtained. Throw off the snares and tap the head with a drum stick about 2" in from each rod, and determine if the pitch is the same at each rod. If not, true it up all around. Then turn the drum over and test the snare head. Here test for tension close to the center near the snares. The head should depress a little more than the batter head to a like amount of pressure. If tension is indicated, proceed as in the case of the batter head, remembering that a little less tension is required on the snare head so that it is free to vibrate against the snares.

Now test for pitch with the stick, snares off. This is more difficult to do, as the head will be a little tighter at the snare beds, but it can be accomplished fairly well.

Now, place the drum on the drum stand and try it, snares on, with the sticks to determine the sound and make any minor adjustments required. Don't forget the tension of the snares. Adjust the snares carefully so that the drum "speaks" freely and does not "choke." Experience will help to etermine the best tension, neither too light (producing a hard tone) nor too loose, producing a tubby tone.

Bass Drum

Test with the stick to see if tension is required. Much has been written about tuning the bass drum. Remember that we are *not* concerned with definite pitch here. The word "bass" is pertinent, however, and the tone should be "dark" and low in pitch. Obviously, the size of the drum is a factor here. For concert, the heads should be low in pitch, many drummers using a low G as a guide to about the correct tension. The drum, again, should be separate tension. If the low G guide is used, tune both heads to approximately this pitch by turning each screw one-half turn, going around the drum clockwise. Then "iron out" the head by placing the palms of the hands one on each head and pressing firmly, to assure that the heads are not sticking to the shell. Retest the tension until the tone is the one desired. Remember the word BASS. The tone should be low, round, and full; thus be careful that the head is not too tight. Tension both heads alike.

Here again personal preference enters into the picture. Some professional bass drummers prefer the beating head several tones higher than the opposite head to minimize what they call "BARK," or "kickback." This is a matter of preference.

All agree that the tone should be low, and dark in quality; and with careful attention to even tension, these qualities can be had, provided the bass drum is of the proper size for the size of the musical organization.

Tympani

Here we are dealing with definite pitch. We will consider the standard pair of 28" and 25" head diameter, and will assume that modern pedal tympani are used.

First, the heads must have "collars," or sufficient slack to secure the low notes.

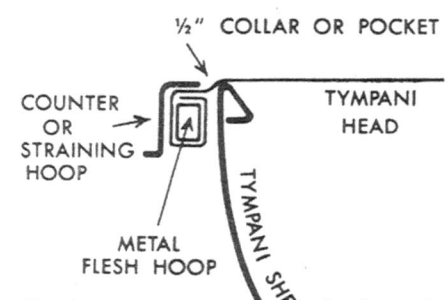

If this collar is present, start with the large kettle, releasing all tension by means of the hand screws, with the pedal in the low note position.. Now begin to apply tension by means of the hand screws to obtain low F.

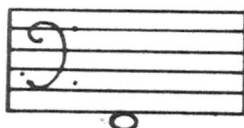

Turn the hand screw in pairs 1 and 4, 2 and 5, 3 and 6, applying only about half a turn on each pair until approximately low F is reached. Then "iron out" the head

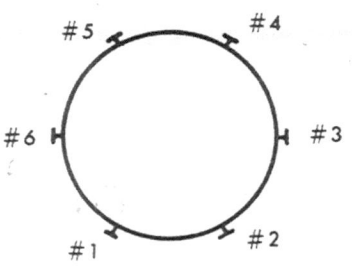

by pressing the center of the head lightly with the palm of the hand several times to remove "slack." Then true up the pitch and test around the drum at each point. Now, press the pedal down to the high note position to be sure the range of a Perfect Fifth is present. The high note on the large drum is C.

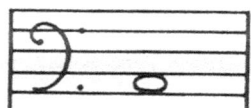

Usually, on good tympani, this top playable note can be had without any difficulty. If, however, the tone is flat, true it up with the hand screws. The drum is now ready for use. Between numbers, occasionally place the pedal in low note position and recheck the low F, making any required adjustments, by means of the hand screws.

Follow the same procedure with the small drum, the low note here being:

    B Flat   The high note F

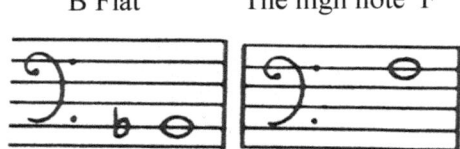

The Care of Drum Heads (Amrawco bulletin, 1963)

The cardinal rule of drum head care can be briefly stated: *"LEAVE THEM ALONE AS MUCH AS POSSIBLE."*

The old saying, "It ain't the heat, it's the humidity," is very true with drum heads. Remember it is the amount of moisture in the air that causes drum heads to tighten or loosen, not the temperature alone, although excessive heat should be avoided.

Another basic rule is: *DO NOT LOOSEN DRUM HEAD AFTER THE DRUM IS USED.* This applies to any drum head. The following suggestions will help to give good drum head service.

Snare Drum

Let us assume the drum is taken from the case for rehearsal or concert, and testing shows it working well, with perhaps only a little tension added during playing time. Play it *as is*, and when finished, leave *as is*, placing back in the case. The next time it is taken from the case, let's say it is a damp day, and the heads are loose. Adjust to playing tension carefully, say a half turn of each rod, and before the rehearsal or concert is concluded, another half turn of each rod is required. In this case, release the same amount of tension added, one turn of each rod, after using. The next time the drum is used, readjust according to the weather, remembering that the least adjustment required the better the results.

If the reverse condition exists and the weather is extremely dry and the drum heads are too tight, release a little tension until playing level is reached, and when finished, leave it alone untul the next use.

Remember this! There are days when it will not. Weather affects drum heads quickly and surely, so allowances must be made for this. With slight adjustments, the drum head can be tightened or loosened to suit the conditions.

Bass Drum

Again, adjust the bass to suit upon use; but due to the low pitch used, after rehearsal or concert, *TIGHTEN* the heads a little (say two tones higher), as the bass drum is used with less tension on the heads. If left in this manner, the heads may well shrink if the weather is dry, and finally have no slack left. Then it will be impossible to loosen the heads enough to secure the pitch desired. If tension is added after use, the head may be quite tight next time the drum is used; however, this is satisfactory, and these is no danger of breakage if good heads are used, and the excessive tension can be released for use. Remember the bass drum is an important MUSIC INSTRUMENT and requires care and attention just as any other instrument. Like tympani heads, there must be a 1/2" collar of head over the edge of the shell of the bass drum.

To expand a bit on the advice regarding detuning after usage– the following comments are from George Way, written in 1916 when he was operating the Advance Drum Company in Edmonton, Alberta:

Should a Drum Head Be Loosened After Using?

Yes and no. It is NOT the heat and the cold that affect a head– as many drummers believe– but it is the *condition* of the heat and cold, or, in other words, it is the dampness and the dryness. A damp cold will loosen a head as well as a damp heat; and a dry cold will tighten a head as well as a dry heat. If you have tightened your drum in damp weather, be sure to let it out when finished to allow for the take-up of the dryness to come in the turning of the weather, of in placing the drum in a very dry place, otherwise the head may burst. Do not continue to tighten a drum in damp weather more than one or two turns; it will continue to "go down" and you will only pull the drum out of shape and nesscessitate the retucking of the heads. The very nature of a head causes this. There is no such thing as an easy-working, tight drum head in damp weather, unless dried out by artificial means. When the heads are tight and working to suit you, leave them alone as much as possible. NEVER loosen the snares when not in use; leave them at a tension, the same as a violin player leaves the strings of his violin. They will then retain "life" and "lay."

CONFLICTING INFORMATION

Since we are looking back and well over a hundred years of published advice on how to best prepare and maintain what is a product of nature, it is not surprising that there are occasionally conflicting words of advice. While most published procedures specify that the water to be used for soaking calf skins prior to tucking should be cool, the Rogers company specified that the water should be luke warm (but not hot.) Leedy once cautioned in an issue of the Leedy Drum Topics that water should be cool and clean; not hot and not cold. Hot or even warm water, they said, will ruin a head immediately if it is submerged.

"SWEET" AND OTHER SPOTS

Is there a "best place" to play a calfskin head? Why are there translucent spots on my white calf head?

There are differing opinions regarding the "sweet spot." I have met drummers who refuse to accept a skin with any marks on it, and others who maintain that translucent spot is the best place to play.

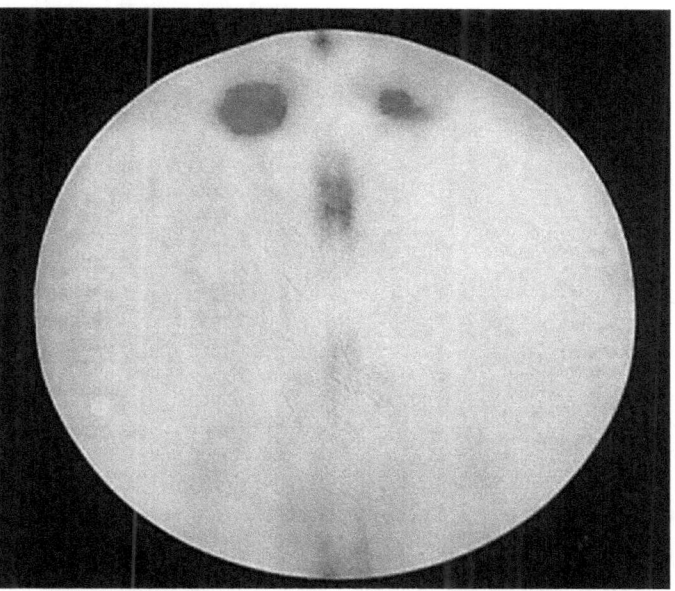

The "spots" on the skin shown above represent the location of the backbone and hip bones. When I once received a skin like this, I phoned Mr. Palansky to ask if this was a defective skin. He explained that the translucent areas were no thinner than the white areas and were not a cause for concern. A Rogers publication from the mid 1920s agrees; "Skins having transparent spots in them are just as good and should not be rejected on this account."

I once addressed a similar concern to noted Timpani expert Rebecca Kite, and she responded with the following comments: *"In choosing a beating spot before mounting the head on the drum, you look for an area where the skin is thin and has few vein marks. Generally this is one of the four spots next to the backbone of the skin. This is usually the best beating spot. A calf head is flexible and resilient. As temperature and humidity change and as the head is played, I find it very likely that different areas of the head will sound better at different times. I think this has more to do with the natural material of the head than the drum or the quality of the head."*

Frozen hides in the Leedy cooler

Leedy, Indianapolis, Production

Drum Heads

The Leedy "hide rooms" or drum head department, were for the most part the province of John Gyuka. Gyuka was born October 6, 1880 in Romania. He immigrated to the United States in 1906 and immediately joined Leedy. He was a close personal friend of U.G. Leedy's and a frequent dinner guest in the Leedy household. Most meals at the Leedy household were served with "UKA" homemade wine that John had been making since his boyhood in the old country. Gyuka supervised each stage of head processing. Hides were frozen as soon as they were received, to keep them from rotting while they awaited processing. They were next submerged in vats where they were deliberately allowed to rot enough for the hair and flesh to be scraped off. Finally, the heads were cut to size and carefully scraped to a uniform thickness. Gyuka became especially well known for developing the world's top class of transparent heads for tympani, which were used by almost every prominent tympanist in the major orchestras of his day.

Just about the time that George Way joined Leedy in 1922, Gyuka left Leedy and went to Kansas City, Missouri, where he started his own head company. Kansas City Rawhide was incorporated by John Gyuka, Carl Hansing, and Harry Hansing in 1922 with a capitalization of $7000.00. U.G. Leedy mentioned in a letter of November 3, 1922 to George Way that he'd just received a notification letter from Gyuka about the new firm with a price list. The prices were at least 10% higher than the Chicago firms. This was a short-lived venture; Gyuka was back in Indianapolis working for Leedy again by 1924. While Leedy catalogs prior to this time had referred to "an expert foreman," Gyuka had not been mentioned by name. Beginning with the Leedy catalog N (which would have been the first catalog published after Gyuka's return) Gyuka was mentioned by name.

Gyuka would move with Leedy to Elkhart in 1930 and remain there for the rest of his life. He passed in 1954 and is buried in Elkhart's Rice Cemetary.

John Gyuka (center, in coveralls) supervising skiving

Leedy Topics: *This shows the numerous tanks in which the hides are washed and rewashed many times. It is here that the flesh and hair is removed, also where the hand-skiving is done.*

Leedy Drum Topics: *When the curing is finished the hides are tacked to these large frames for drying and later cut into the various sized circles and sorted for branding. Leedy heads are carried through their entire process of manufacture without damaging the fibres of the hides.*

Head Tucking
Leedy Drum Topics: *Great care is taken to see that all heads are tucked without any greater strain at one point than another. An evenly tucked head assures the same flexibility over its entire surface when dry.*

Art Department
Leedy Drum Topics: *Painting on bass drum heads, so that the work is artistic, is a "trade" all its own. All our engraved shells are high-class hand-work and not of the common machine variety. Mr. Ed Riedwig, our artist, is permanently employed at the factory, as is also Mr. J. F. Hammond, our engraver.*

1920s Leedy Head stamps

premium calf, white, "hard" surface

cheaper skins from South America

budget transparent snare drum head

transparent bass drum, timpani head

premium transparent snare drum head

1930s Leedy Head stamps

1940s Leedy Head stamps

Wm. F. Ludwig II Calf comments

The following is an excerpt from Wm. F. Ludwig II's autobiography The Making Of A Drum Company

The Great Crosstown Head Race

Throughout all of the decade of the 1950s, I was in a car and foot race with Bud Slingerland to get the best calf skin heads for our increasing drum production. There were four sources of supply and we would often find ourselves facing one another in the waiting rooms of one of the drum head tanneries. When that happened, which was often, we exchanged fairly civilized greetings, but there was a feeling of triumph in the breast of whoever got there first! The two main suppliers were American Rawhide Manufacturing Company and the White Eagle Rawhide Manufacturing Company. Each would call us both as nearly simultaneously as possible with the news that a fresh supply of calfskin and slunk heads was assembled for our picking and approval. When I got that call I would drop whatever I was doing and race through the office, coat tails flying, jump into my car and floor it down to that tannery. Arriving ahead of Bud gave me a tremendous feeling of jubilation since I would then go through the stacks of freshly tanned heads picking out only the best and leaving the poorest for Bud. The same happened if Bud won the race. Gretsch came in third since they were preoccupied with guitars and their general jobbing business downtown on Wabash avenue.

Selecting heads involved holding each one up to the light to search for salt stains which would discolor the heads on the drum. Also we held the edges between both hands and passed the head completely around the circumference searching for evenness in thickness. A thin head would be good for snare drums and a thick one for parade drums.

It was at about this time that our sales manager, Fred Miller, changed our nomenclature from "field" drums to "parade" drums as these drums were no longer used on the field but on parade.

Calf heads were tanned from yearling calves less than a year in age. Slunk skins were tanned from unborn calfskins which, as gruesome as it sounds, were often by products of the cow slaughtering process. These slunk skins were also used for many other products such as fine leather men's and ladies' gloves. Since cattle were sold to the slaughter houses by weight, farmers did not hesitate to sell pregnant cows for meat and the unborn calf became a profitable by-product. Naturally the slunk skins were extremely undeveloped and therefore thin and ideal for snare heads. Because of the economy of this process, there were always far more slunk snare drum heads available than calf batter heads. But I had to beware! Very often there were tiny pin holes in the head which could only be discovered by holding the skins up to a light. Slunk skins had to be carefully selected and if Bud was in the waiting room, I took extra care and time to leave him as many pin-holed slunk skins and salt-stained batter heads as possible. He did likewise, thus the "Great Cross Town Races"!

Timpani heads were particularly difficult to choose for the highest quality assuring the performer the very best sound. One professional timpanist in particular, Cloyd Duff of the Cleveland Symphony Orchestra, would order six timpani heads each summer directly from my father who would then begin to go through stacks of timpani heads looking for only the special, special best. When he had six even transparent calf skin heads he would ship them. Duff would then pick out four and return two! This careful head selection made our drums sound better and look better as well. Each drum was tuned to play at the end of the assembly line and then packed for shipment. Every timpano was hand-fitted with the appropriate thickness calf skin head for the particular size timpano by my Dad or me. For instance, the smaller-sized timpani were fitted with thicker heads to provide more body. Otherwise, the small diameter of the kettle would sound thin to the ears. Larger diameters of timpani were fitted with thinner heads to enhance a quicker response to the sticks. You would expect larger to be thicker and smaller to be thinner, but no; it was the other way around; larger sizes were thinner than smaller sizes. That was the way it was for the final decade of the calf skin era which, unknown to everyone, was rapidly coming to a close. With the close of that era, a certain competitive advantage would be lost.

Leedy & Ludwig calf head production, 1953

Having purchased both the Leedy Company and the Ludwig Company around 1930, Conn for over twenty years produced both brands of drums. The two divisions were combined in 1951, creating the "Leedy-Ludwig" drum company. The following procedures (from the archives of the late George Way,) were used by Leedy & Ludwig to produce calfskin heads.

COMPLETE OPERATIONS AND METHOD TO CONVERT CALF SKINS INTO WHITE CALF BASS AND WHITE CALF BATTER HEADS

Operation
1. Unload and weigh skins.
2. Trim head and shanks and split tail.
3. Soak in Soaking Tank for 24 hours, using clear cold water.
4. Green Fleshing thru fleshing machine, once from the head and once from the tail.
5. Soak in Soaking Tank for 24 hours, using clear, cold water.
6. Soak in lime solution to loosen hair– using paddle wheel vats. Lime solution to be made of clear cold water and 1/2 lb. lump lime for each calf skin. Paddle wheels to be turned at least twice each day until hair is sufficiently loose to remove by hand. Length of time depends on temperature- approximately 3 to 4 days in summer and 4 to 5 days in winter.
7. Place skins in barrel, using warm water about 80 degrees, ready for beamsters to unhair.
8. Unhair on beam.
9. Split heads of skins– using splitting machine.
10. Relime skins in barrel for 48 hours, using 10 lbs lump lime per 100 skins.
11. Lime fleshing thru fleshing machine, twice from head and twice from tail.
12, Wash skins in mill using 1 lb. XXA Oropon placed in a bag for each 100 lbs of finished hides. Use clear warm water about 90 degrees, running mill for 10 minutes. Soak for 1 hour without mill running, repeating operation of running mill and soaking four times.
13. Drain bate from mill and run mill 1/2 hour, using clear cold water to wash Oropon from skins.
14. Drain cold water and run mill for 15 minutes, using warm water about 90 degrees.
15. Bleaching operation- drain sufficient warm water from mill so that water just covers skins, adding 5 qts Hydrogen of Peroxide for 250 skins. Run mill for 15 minutes. Soak in mill without running for 1 hour. Run mill 15 minutes and soak in Peroxide solution overnight.
16. Wash in clear cold water, running mill for 30 minutes.
17. Tack skin on wood tacking boards, stretching skin with pliers during the tacking operation.
18. Place on steam pipes to dry. Heat is necessary in the drying operation for White Calf heads.
19. Remove from tacking frame.
20. Select heavy skins for bass drum heads and light skins for Batter Heads.
21. Mark for size.
22. Cut.
23. Bass drum heads to be buffed, using Buffing Machine.
24. Batter heads to be shaved to even thickness by hand shaver.
25. Batter heads to be buffed.
26. Wipe both sides of all heads with a solution consisting of 5 tablespoons of Gum of Tragacanth in 3 gallons of water.

Most suitable skins for White Calf Bass and Batter heads are selected large packers 8 lb. and down light calf. These skins should be in salt pack for at least 2 weeks to be thoroughly cured before using.

COMPLETE OPERATIONS AND METHOD TO CONVERT HAIRLESS SLUNK SKINS INTO TRANSPARENT SNARE SIDE HEADS

Operation
1. Unload and count skins
2. Trim head and shanks
3. Soak in cold clear water over night
4. Green fleshing through fleshing machine, once from head and once from tail.
5. Soak in clear cold water for beamsters.
6. Remove grain on beam.
7. Soak in clear cold water until 500 are accumulated.
8. Place in mill, running 15 minutes, using clear cold water. Drain water until skins are just covered; add 1/2 pint of Sulphuric Acid for 500 skins, running mill for 15 minutes. Wash in clear cold water, running mill for 20 minutes.
9. Tack on wood tacking frames. Skins must be tacked loose and not stretched for transparent skins.
10. Place skins in Sulphur Room, burning suplhur for 15 minutes.
11. Place in drying room without hea.
12. Remove skins from tacking frames
13. Mark to size
14. Cut to size
15. Sort, clean, and pack.

Use large packer fresh hairless slunk skins measuring 16" and over across narrow portion of skin. Skins measuring 14" to 16" are graded as #2 and should be purchased at half price. Skins measuring under 14" or skins with cuts are graded as glues and are not to be purchased.

COMPLETE OPERATIONS AND METHOD TO CONVERT HAIRLESS SLUNK SKINS INTO WHITE SLUNK BATTER HEADS

OPERATION - Select heavy skins from the lot of hairless slunks
1. Unload and count skins.
2. Trim head and shanks.
3. Soak in cold water over night.
4. Green fleshing thru fleshing machine, once from head and once from tail.
5. Soak in clear cold water for beamsters.
6. Remove grain onbeam.
7. Place in lime solution in 50-gal. barrel, using 2 1/2 over twice a day for 5 minutes.
8. Lime fleshing thru fleshing machine.
9. Bleaching operation. Place 100 skins in 50-gal. barrel, using 1 Gal. of Hydrogen of Peroxide and soak over night.
10. Wash in clear cold water for 15 minutes.
11. Place in new lime solution using 2 1/2 lbs of lump lime in 50-gal. barrel, soaking for 24 hours. Skins to be turned over 3 to 4 times.
12. Tack on tacking boards, skins to be stretched for White Slunks.
13. Place on steam pipes to dry, heat being necessary to dry White Slunks.
14. Remove from tacking frames.
15. Mark to size.
16. Cut to size.
17.. Buff, using buffing machine.

COMPLETE OPERATIONS AND METHOD TO CONVERT CALF SKINS INTO WHITE CALF BANJO HEADS

Operations 1 to 16 similar to converting Calkf Skins into White Calf Bass and Batter Heads.

OPERATION

17. Place in lime solution in barrell, using 10 lbs of lump lime for 50 skins; soak for 48 hours, turning skins over twice a day for 10 minutes each time.
18. Stretch on peg type stretching frames, with head of skin up and tail down. All stretch possible must be taken out of skin to avoid transparent spots.
19. Shave with moon knife on flesh side.
20. Remove skin from frame,
21. Mark to size, making certain that the flank part of the skin is not used in the #1 heads.
22. Cut to size.
23. Shave by hand to even thickness.
24. Buff, using buffing machine.
25. Wipe both sides of head with Gum of Tragcanth solution.

Use fresh large packer calf skins weighing 10 to 12 lbs.

COMPLETE OPERATIONS AND METHOD TO CONVERT CALF SKINS INTO TRANSPARENT TYMPANI HEADS.

Select skins of even thickness, without defects such as cuts or scars.

Operations 1 to 11 similar to converting Calf Skins into White Calf Bass and Batter heads.

OPERATION
12. Shave head on beam for even thickness.
13. Wash skins in mill, using 1 Lb. XXA Oropon placed in a bag for each 100 lbs. of finished hides. Use clear warm water about 90 degrees, running mill for 10 minutes. Soak for 1 hour without mill running, repeating operation of running mill and soaking 4 times.
14. Drain bate from mill and run mill 1/2 hour, using clear cold water to wash Oropon from skins.
15. Drain cold water and run mill for 15 minutes, using warm water about 90 degrees.
16. Drain sufficient water from mill so that water just covers skins, adding 1 pint of Sulphuric Acid per 100 skins. Run mill for 15 minutes. Add cold water while mill is running for 1/2 hour and drain.
17. Take skins from mill and hang on hooks in Sulphur Room, burning sulphur for 15 minutes.
18. Soak in clear cold water in barrel over night.
19. Tack skins on clean wood tacking frames, skin to be tacked loose and not stretched for transparent head.
20. Place in drying room without heat; natural drying is necessary on transparent tympani heads as heat tends to turn skins white..
21. Remove skin from tacking frame.
22. Mark for size.
23. Cut to size.
24. Shave by hand to even thickness.
25. Wipe both sides of heads with gum of Tragacanth solution.

ABOUT DRUM HEADS
originally published by the Leedy & Ludwig drum division of the C.G. Conn Company, circa 1952

HOW TO TUCK DRUM HEADS

The best results are obtained by soaking the head in clear cool water about ten munites for snare drum and twenty minutes fo bass drum. Be sure the water is not warm because warm water will shrink and ruin any drum head. Neither should the water be too cold. Also be sure the water is clean. Soapy or greasy water will ruin a drum head. Do not under any circumstances wrinkle the drum head to force it into too small a container. Be sure the container is long enough to lay the whole head in without crushing.

After head has become soft and pliable it should be laid hair (smooth) side down and flesh (rough) side up on a smooth table. Smooth out with the palm of the hand until it lies flat and even without wrinkles. Wipe off all water on both sides, turning head several times.

Next, lay the flesh hoop centrally on the head as shown in Figure 1, allowing an equal margin all around for tucking. It may be necessary to trim the head down to the proper size to allow enough margin so the head may be tucked in under the flesh hoop. A sharp knife or scissors is suitable for this purpose but be sure not to leave ragged edges– make a perfect circle.

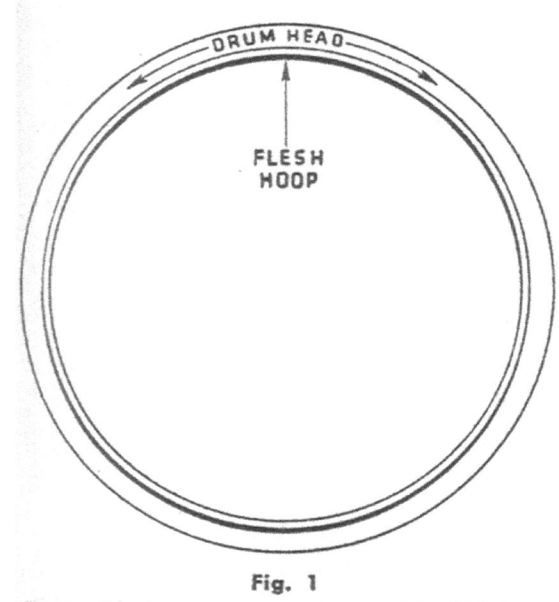

Fig. 1

The best tucking tool is one made for the purpose as shown in Figure 2. However, if one of these is not available a tablespoon handle will suffice provided the end is round and smooth. Be sure it is not sharp enough to cut the head.

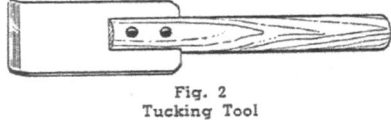

Fig. 2
Tucking Tool

Begin tucking at point marked No. 1 in Figure 3. The head should be carefully folded over the hoop and tucked under the lower inside edge two or two and one-half inches in length. Next take the same kind of a tuck at point marked No. 2 directly opposite on the circle; then do the same thing at points No. 3 and No. 4. Be careful not to stretch the head unevenly in any direction from the center. Continue to follow the diagram of Figure 3, next tucking at points 5,6,7 and 8, keeping the even stretching in mind all of the time. Do not pull too hard or you will cause wrinkles. Following this the balance of the head may be tucked at points opposite each other as you continue.

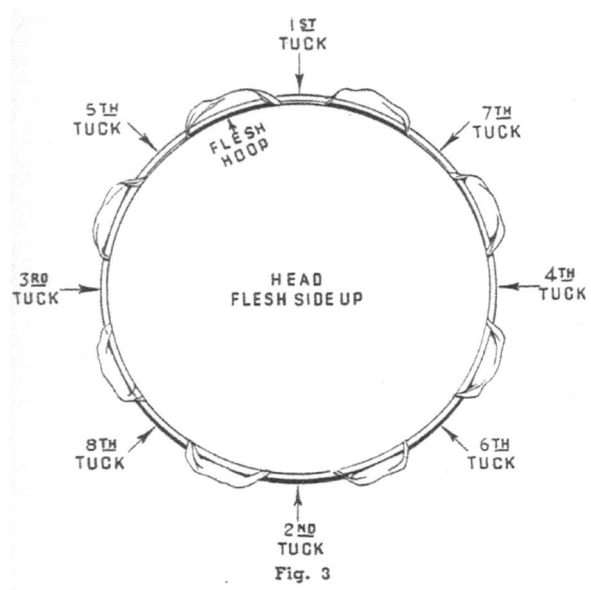

Fig. 3

On WOOD flesh hoops it is not absolutely necessary to push the head beyond the outside bottom edge of the flesh hoop. There is a certain amount of natural glue in all hides which naturally adheres to the wood flesh hoop. On METAL flesh hoops, however, it is necessary to push the head over the outside edge of the metal flesh hoop and upward, as described in Figure 4. Do not tuck on metal flesh hoops as shown in Figure 5 or the head may slip off the metal hoop.

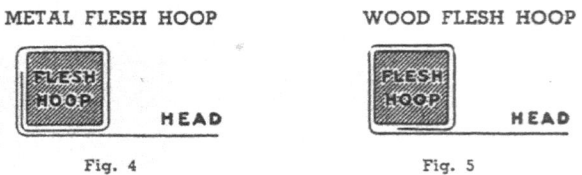

Fig. 4 Fig. 5

Figure 6 shows how the tool is used to shove the head beyond the outside edge for metal flesh hoops mentioned above. There may be a little bulk where the head is shoved through to the outside edge, leaving a ridge, but this does not show when the flesh hoop is in place within the Floating Head counter hoop. This style of tucking assures it will hold better.

Many tuckers make the mistake of putting the head on the drum shell and adjusting the hoops and rods in place while the head is wet. Do not do this. It is O.K. to place the head (after it is tucked,) on the shell without first drying, but WITHOUT the hoops and rods.

White heads should dry fast, as stretching does not discolor them, but transparent or clear heads should dry very slowly so there will be no fast stretching. When transparent heads dry fast they stretch unduly and often turn white at various points.

Bass drum heads are much heavier and stronger thatn snare drum heads; therefore, it is O.K. to put the hoops and rods in place while the head is wet and pulled down slightly!

ABOUT METAL FLESH HOOPS

Heads may be tucked on metal flesh hoops and carried indefinitely without the hoop becoming warped. This is agreat advantage when it becomes necessary to make a quick change. When tucking a head on a metal flesh hoop, let it become THOROUGHLY dry before putting on drum shell. Heads will never slip off metal flesh hoops if they are correctly tucked. Be sure to shove the head ALL THE WAY under the flesh hoop, allowing a little to go BEYOND the outside corner as show in figures 4 and 6. Never tuck a metal hoop as shown in figure 5.

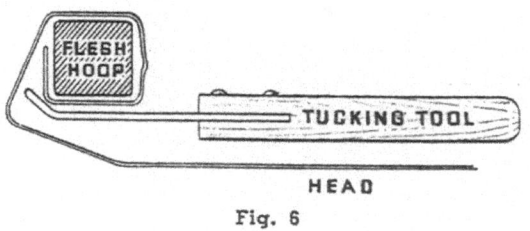

Fig. 6

HOW TO TUCK TYMPANI HEADS

Soak tympani heads in clear cool water for about twenty minutes. It takes some heads longer than others to become soft and pliable. Be sure the water is not warm. Warm water will ruin any drum head. Pleace head on smooth table with the hair side down and flesh side up. The procedure for tucking on the metal tympani hoop is practically the same as described for tucking snare drum heads on our metal Floating Head hoop. However, timpani heads MUST BE TUCKED QUITE LOOSE! Place a twelve-inch wooden chopping bowl or something of a similar design on the table under the head. This will give the slack required but be sure not to stretch the head unevenly in any direction from the center toward the hoop. After you have finished tucking all the way around the hoop, remove the bowl and smooth the wrinkled spots on the head out with your tucking tool by rubbing it gently along the sides of the flesh hoop. Be sure to tuck the head clear around the hoop to the under side as shown in Figure 4. This is important.

Next, place the head on the tympani bowl but do not put the counter hoop or tension handles in place. Allow the head to dry slowly. After the head is dry, put on the counter hoop and tension handles; then slowly pull down the handles. If the head is too tight, remove from the kettle bowl and sponge on both sides with a damp cloth to provide more slack. Replace on bowl and pull down to obtain a "collar." See Figure 7. (The "collar" is the portion of the head which bends downward over the edge at the bowl.) Repeat this until you have obtained a full half inch "collar." When the head is thoroughly dry you will have sufficient slack or "back up" to always obtain low notes.

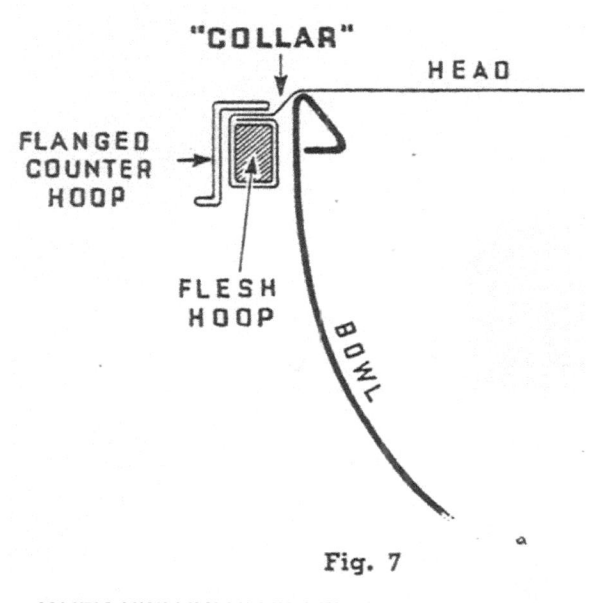

Fig. 7

Good tympany heads should be very "elastic." Transparent heads, otherwise known as "clear" heads, are more elastic than white heads. That is why they are used on timpani. Clear heads will stretch and contract more than the white type and therefore produce maximum tonal quality and resonant volume. The fact that timpani heads often contract so that low notes cannot be reached proves in itself that they are good heads.

When a head becomes too tight to reach the low notes it is wholly due to a misunderstanding of how to handle same. The portion of the head which turns downward over the edge of the timpani bowl is called the "collar." A reasonable amount of "collar" must be kept on the tympani head at all times so that there is enough "let out" to reach the lower notes.

When the player is through using the instruments the pedals, if they are pedal timpani, should be left up as HIGH as they will go. This should put slack in the heads. Then the tension handles should be turned until there is at least a half inch "collar" over the edge of the bowl. Of course this will mean that at times the heads will be very tight when not in use, but if they are tensioned evenly there is no danger of breaking providing they are TOP QUALITY heads.

If it is impossible to obtain the "collar" because because the heads are dried out and too tight, remove the heads from the tympani and then sponge them carefully with a damp–not soaking wet–cloth on both sides to within an inch and a half of the flesh hoop. Be sure you do not get the water in under the hoop. Next place the head back on the kettle and strain slowly and evenly so that you will have a quarter inch "collar." Allow to dry slowly. Take off the head again and repeat until you have obtained the full half inch "collar." In the future keep this "collar" on the heads when the instruments are not in use. This is the procedure followed by all of the large symphony orchestra and concert band timpanists.

When next used, the handles of the small kettle should be loosened evenly until the note B-flat is reached. On the large kettle the handles should be loosened until the note F is reached. If you have kept the pedal up as high as it will go while you were tuning to these notes with the handles, you will find that you have the full scope of the pedal for the notes on up the scale as the pedal is pressed downward. Then when the pedal is raised again it will be a very easy matter to reach the low notes.

A DRUM HEAD FACT

It is NOT heat and cold alone that affect snare and bass drum heads– it is the condition of the heat and cold, viz: dampness and dryness. A damp head will cause the head to slacken, and the same with a damp cold. A dry heat will cause a head to tighten, and the same with a dry cold. Therefore, watch the condition of the atmosphere rather than the thermometer, and avoid head breakage. If you have tightened your head on a damp night, let it out after using to the point where you started to take it up. This will allow some slack for a "take-up" should the next day be dry. If your drum works nicely in dry weather, let it alone. By following this tip you will save many heads and many dollars!

MORE ABOUT DRUM HEADS

The age of the animal (calf) determines the thickness of a drum head.

Transparent or clear heads such as Leedy & Ludwig "Uka" snare heads (also called "slunk,") are the hides of unborn calves.

White heads such as used on the batter side of orchestra, band, and street drums– Leedy & Ludwig "Standard" Hardwhite and "Superior" hardwhite– are taken from calves three to five weeks old.

The average white bass drum head is from calves five to nine weeks old.

Tympani heads also are from calves from five to nine weeks old.

One of the main processes in making heads white is even stretching during their manufacture. Transparent heads are hides in their natural state and not stretched; they are, therefore, more elastic than the white heads and better for the snare side of a drum and for tympani where maximum vibration is required.

Hides are never "split" for manufacturing drum heads, as many believe. Each head is made from the natural thickness. There is only one average size head in the "slunk" of transparent type.

Sometimes two and three white batter heads are obtained from a single hide, it being large enough for circles to be cut from the hide.

Bass drum and tympani heads are from a single hide.

PRESENTED BY

Leedy & Ludwig

DIVISION OF C. G. CONN LTD.
"The World's Finest Drummers' Instruments Since 1895"

Ludwig Calf heads

This page and the next are excerpted from The Ludwig Book by Rob Cook, a Rebeats publication

1922–1930 Ludwig & Ludwig Drum Head facility on Elston Avenue. This was the world's largest and most modern drum head facility, located near the Ludwig factory, in an area zoned for animal processing. At about the same time that Conn bought Ludwig this building was condemned to make way for a new bridge. Conn produced heads for Leedy and Ludwig & Ludwig in a new Elkhart tannery with Leedy personnel.

(The photo above and caption below are from a 1922 Ludwig catalog)
Superintendent of our drum head plant is Mr. Lucian Bon Christiano; inventor of the alligator process and a thorough and practical drum head maker. Mr. Christiano is a professional drummer as well, a member of the Federation of Musicians and well known in the profession as a drummer.

1912–1919 General range of calf heads.
1920–1923 Tympani heads

1917-1927

1928-1939

1940-1949

Transparent heads; thin and medium for snare-side, heavy for batter side.

1920–1949
When this series was introduced, the "Selected Special" oval (above) became the timpani designation until introduction of the Vellour timpani heads.

1922–1925
Transparent calfskin heads for snare or batter sides, specially treated to resist moisture. (NOT made from Alligator.)

1927-1947

1948–1949

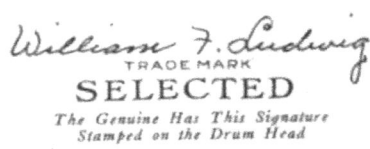
1924–1927

1928–1931, 1939–1947

1932–35

1937–1938

Introduced as a premium brand, the signature series was a step up from the Ludwig Whitecalf, above; tighter fiber and smoother grain.

1948-1949

Leedy & Ludwig calf heads 1951–1955

WFL calf heads 1948–1955

Ludwig 1956–70 (The 1972 catalog mentions that calf heads will still be supplied upon special request but are no longer catalogued due to the popularity of plastic heads.)

Early Days of Rogers

Joseph H. Rogers learned his trade as a boy in the parchment yards of Dublin, Ireland. He immigrated to the United States in 1840, and in 1849 established what is reputed to be the country's first drum head factory. The most reliable sources available indicate that the first Rogers calfskin head facility was set up in Brewster's Station, New York, moving later to Danbury, Connecticut, and finally to Highview, New York. It was here that Rogers began to establish an international reputation as a supplier of top quality calfskin drum heads. Up until this time nearly all banjo heads had been made from sheepskin, which was easier to treat in terms of equipment, materials, and knowledge. Sheepskins, because they contain very little natural glue, wear more quickly and lose their tone from the constant pounding of the drum sticks. Although the prices of Rogers calf heads were higher, customers gladly paid extra to get the superior performance.

Joseph H. Rogers

Joseph H. Rogers Sr. won a blue ribbon, a bronze medal, and a citation at the World's Columbian Exposition in Chicago in 1893.

When Joseph Rogers died he left the operation to his son Joseph H. Rogers Junior (born in 1856) who maintained a tannery in Highview but moved his base of operations and opened a second tannery in Farmingdale, New Jersey in 1909. (Actually the facility was about a mile outside of downtown Farmingdale, "West of the center of town on the road to Ardena.") The standards of excellence established by Joseph Rogers Sr. were maintained by the family. By the early 1920s, Rogers heads were shipped as standard equipment on all of the finest banjos made by Gibson, Vega, George B. Stone, Walberg & Auge, Odell, M. Chapman, Wm. L. Lange (Paramount,) Weymann & Son, Bacon, and dozens of others. Rogers heads were not the cheapest, but were without question the finest. Even drum companies that eventually opened their own tanneries continued to catalogue Rogers drum heads as a premium option.

Joseph H. Rogers Junior

The banjo (and drum) head business was very lucrative for the Rogers family, particularly the first two generations. The fact that their heads were priced higher did not indicate that they were making more profit per head, since they had to spend more for premium skins to process. They sold far more heads than any of their competitors. The firm produced leather products in addition to drum heads; leather coverings for heavy books, as well as coverings for artificial arms and legs. Though the firm employed only about eight employees, they processed up to 500 skins per day. (One fair-sized skin could yield up to 8 heads.) Employees of the 1940s (when production was tapering off) remember that the Pennsylvania Railroad was still a major transporter of the skins. Large tractor-trailors would pull in weekly, and literally tons of skins would be unloaded into huge vats directly below the main head processing building in Farmingdale.

Joseph H. Rogers Junior left the business to two sons, Joseph B. Rogers and Cleveland S. Rogers.

The blue ribbon and bronze medal awarded to Joseph H. Rogers at the 1883 Colombian Exposition in Chicago.

ROGERS CALF SKIN HEADS
reprinted from "The Rogers Book," by Rob Cook

There were two basic reasons why Rogers skin heads were superior to any competition. They were made from the very finest materials available, and the processes & workmanship of the manufacturing process were unparalleled. As the Rogers catalogs of the 1930s pointed out, there were many skin heads on the market to choose from. These included:

Sheep skin Rogers cautioned their customers that some of their competitors made their heads from sheep skin and represented them as calf skin. These hides contained little or no glue and wore out quickly.

Goat skin Another inferior hide which, according to Rogers, was often sold as genuine calf skin. Like sheep skin, this material was inferior in quality to calfskin.

Veal calf The highest grade of calf skin, veal calf came from cattle which were fed only milk from the cow. This type of feeding provided the calf with "an excellent and healthy constitution thereby eliminating imperfections usually attendant in calves fed by other means." These hides were plump and tight-fibered. Rogers applied their name only to heads made from veal calf hides.

Patent feed calf Slightly inferior in quality to the veal calf hides, these hides came from calves that were fed by the farmer; patented feeds, skim milk, or buttermilk.

Pasture calf The lowest grade of hide, from calves allowed to graze in the pastures.

Grades of Rogers Heads, 1938

Three Star Brand, Superior Brand The "ultimate" head; the very best that Rogers was capable of producing. Three Star Brand heads were from Farmingdale, Superior Brand were from Highview.

Union Brand, First Quality Brand The next step down from Three Star and Superior. Rogers described these heads as "superior in every respect to competitive makes" and warranteed them to be free from flaws and defects. First Quality Brand heads were from Farmingdale, Union Brand heads were from Highview.

Daisy Brand These heads were slightly off in color (the heads above were all guarenteed to be all white) or bearing some other slight defect which was "not detrimental to either wearing qualities or tone value."

Soo Brand These heads were not stamped with the Rogers name or bleached white; a budget head, though still made from veal calfskin.

Earliest known Rogers catalog; head booklet, mid 1920s

Highview, NY tannery stamp

Farmingdale, NJ tannery stamp

Processing the skins

The truckloads of skins were received pretty much free of flesh, but with hair. The heads were unloaded from the trucks directly into large soaking vats, where they soaked for two days.

When the skins came out of their initial soaking bath, they were put on a barrel-like board where the remaining flesh was removed and the rough edges were trimmed. They were next put into the "secret chemical bath," perfected by Rogers, for two weeks. This conditioned the skin and removed a lot of the hair. Now the skins were ready to be stretched onto drying frames.

Stretching skin onto drying rack

As soon as the skins were mounted on the drying frames, they were placed in the drying room for 24 hours. Former employees remember that they had to walk through the drying room to get to the office, and that the temperature there was kept over 80 degrees Farenheit year-round.

Shaving the skin

When the skins were removed from the drying room after 24 hours, they were scraped again. By this point, the procedures were done only by qualified and experienced workmen. One of the main "skin scrapers" for many years was William E. Gravatt. Cleveland Rogers' niece Marylyn loved to visit the factory because the Gravatts lived right across the road and had a daughter Marjorie's age she could play with. This daughter always fascinated Marylyn because she had an extra thumb. Gravatt's son Robert W. Gravatt also worked for Rogers for a few years.

Drying the skins outdoors

After the skins left the drying room and were scraped, they were taken outside to the drying field. Rogers prided themselves on the fact that the sun and open air bleached their heads, while other companies resorted to chemicals. This procedure took longer and was more costly, but this was part of the reason Rogers heads were more durable.

The dried heads were now ready for a final scraping. This final scraping was the most delicate stage of the entire process. Skilled workmen used 14-pound half-moon shaving knives with razor-sharp feather-edge blades to scrape the skins to a uniform thickness. It took workers at least three years to reach this level of skill which paid the top salary in the factory. This scraping was done in a clean room where the white shavings were carefully preserved and sold for use as gelatin stock.

Finally the scraped skins were removed from the racks and sent to the cutting bench where workers could produce over 400 heads per day.

It is unclear whether competitors did not know how to produce white heads using natural processes the way Rogers did or whether they found it neccessary to speed the process up. For whatever reason, they used chemicals in the whitening stage– usually sulfuric acid and hydrogen or sodium peroxide. (The more delicate "slunk" heads made from the hides of unborn calves and used for the snare side heads of snare drums were placed in a room with burning sulfer for less than an hour.) These processes resulted in heads of lesser quality than Rogers.

BOVID PERCUSSION

Leaving the hair on a hide that is made into a drum head yields both a unique tone and a unique appearance. All of the skins on these pages are one-of-a-kind. Bovid provides calf, goat, camel, and steer heads.

Bovid heads are tucked on cold-rolled solid aluminum flesh hoops. A unique offering from Bovid are multi-ply skin heads which offer unique tones and increased durability.

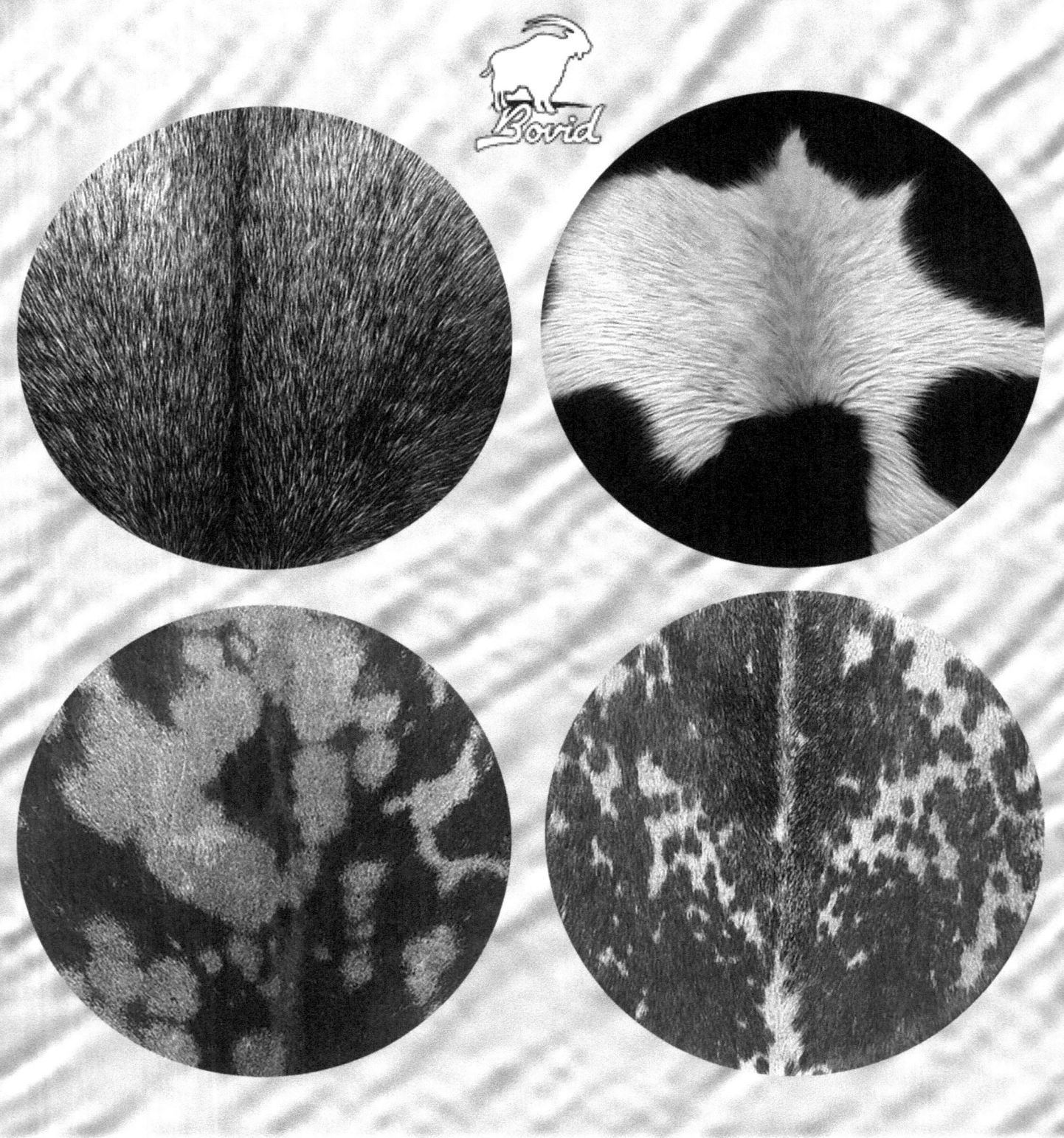

BOVID PERCUSSION

PAINTED BASS DRUM HEADS

Leedy employed Mr. Ed. Riedwig, above, was their full-time artist painting bass drum heads.
(They also employed an engraver, Mr. J.F. Hammond.)

photo courtesy of Timothy Northrup, Northrup Drum Museum   www.northrupgallery.com

LEEDY PAINTED BASS DRUM HEADS

Leedy took great pride in their painted drum heads. These oil paintings were done by hand by talented and experienced artists. They used a "stipple" method of painting so that no brush marks were visible. It was important that the paintings be done in a "stained glass" style rather than layering the different components, as the bass drums frequently had one or two lights installed which could flash on and off. In addition to the stock images shown here, Leedy also accepted special order paintings from sketches, photos, or pictures from magazines.

Dutch Windmill Scene 1925-1940

Spider Web Girl 1930-1935

Ship Silhouette 1927-1935

Kissing Silhouette 1927

Bathing Girl 1930-1935

Japanese Silhouette 1930-1935

Dancing Girl 1924-1927

Butter Fly Silhouette 1928-1935

Kissing Silhouette 1927

Marine Scene 1924

Harlequin Girl 1930-1935

Venetian Boatman Scene 1925-1927

Indian Scene 1928

Sentinel Silhouette 1928-1935

Japanese Landscape 1924

The last Leedy catalog to feature oil-painted scenes was #44 of 1940. Catalog #45 of 1941 featured these six monogram designs. This was the last catalog to feature any kind of custom drum head art.

Butter Fly Girl 1928-1935

LUDWIG PAINTED BASS DRUM HEADS

Hand-painted with oil on leather, these were true works of art, available for an extra $10.00–$12.00. The appearance of the bass drum could be further enhanced with optional red, blue, and/or frosted white lamps which could be made to blink. Ludwig painted bass drum heads were last pictured in the 1940 catalog and last mentioned in the 1941 catalog when Ludwig offered to paint scenes from sketches, photos, or pictures. Customers were advised to send their artwork so a quote could be prepared.

Mountain & Lake
1924–1940

1927    1930

Winter Scene
1924–1930

1927   1930

Millstream
1929–1940

Jazz Pirates
1926–1932

Windmill
1929–1932

Cabin
1924–1927

Because each head was hand-painted, each was unique. Note the differences between the 1927 and 1930 *Winter Scene* and *Mountain And Lake* paintings. Additionally, customers could special-order personalized oil-painted heads. Because of these factors, it would be virtually impossible to show all head designs and specific production dates. The dates listed here reflect catalog listings, for purposes of generalized dating.

Niagara Falls
1924–1934

Charleston Dancer
1926–1927

Clipper Ship
1928

photo courtesy Billy Jeansonne

Dutch Windmill*
1928–1935

Spanish Dancers*
1926–1939

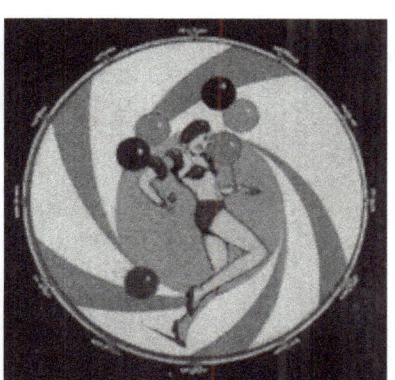

Balloon Dancer*
1935–1940

Other designs listed, but not illustrated here or in catalogs:
Nude Silhouette 1926–1932
Bathing Girl   1926–1932
Pirouette   1926–1927
Clown   1926–1927
Forest Fire   1928–1932
Spirit of St. Louis   1928
Tropical Scene 1924

Lake   1924*

*Catalog illustrations appeared only in black and white, although the oil-paintings were in full color.

SLINGERLAND PAINTED BASS DRUM HEADS

Slingerland's first catalog of 1928 followed the lead of competitors Leedy and Ludwig in offering hand-painted bass drum scenes. The offerings were expanded slightly in the 1934 catalog, shown here. This was the last catalog to offer such scenes.

The Northrup Collection
Photos courtesty of Timothy Northrup, Northrup Drum Museum

Ludwig Moose Drum head never appeared in a catalog except on the Cover of the 1928 catalog on Jack "Peacock" Kelly's drum set

A Walberg & Auge design

Leedy "Kissing Silouette" pattern

Rare "Full Moon" variation of Silouette pattern

Leedy "Spider Web Girl"

(Left) Backlit with lights inside the bass drum

(Right) With no lights

The Polites Collection
photos courtesy of Patrick Polites

Spanish Dancers, with backlighting **Spanish Dancers, no backlighting**

Patrick Polites: "An artist named Iradine Gibson signed 3 known copies of this one and 2 Jazz Pirates. She did coloring on underside as well, and all 3 known copies are colored different. Mine needs back lighting to see most of the colors."

Additional personalization was an option, as seen on these heads from the Polites collection.

The Polites Collection
photos courtesy of Patrick Polites

Leedy " the Harlequin Girl"

Ludwig "Millstream"

A factory "one off" of a nude Spider Girl

The designs illustrated in the catalogs were sort of a stepping off point... the artists often produced variations on those themes.

More Drum Head Information

Using Calf Timpani Heads
by Rebecca Kite
December, 1992,
Percussive Notes

Calf Skin Heads And Bass Drums
by Jack Butcher
June, 1992,
Percussive Notes

Calf Timpani Heads On Tour
by SMSgt. James A. Nierescher
April, 1993,
Percussive Notes

The Art of Tucking Calf Timpany Heads
by Michael Rosen
December, 1995,
Percussive Notes

Mounting Calf Heads On Timpani
by Michael Rosen
April, 1996,
Percussive Notes

The Mylar Drum Head
by Charles "Woody" Thompson
August, 1989,
Modern Drummer

Inside Evans
by William F Miller
March, 1989, Modern Drummer

Inside Remo
by David Levine
April/May, 1980,
Modern Drummer

When Calfskin Was King: Part 1
by Woody Thompson
February, 1993,
Modern Drummer

When Calfskin Was King: Part 2
by Woody Thompson
March, 1993,
Modern Drummer

When Calfskin Was King: Part 3
by Woody Thompson
April, 1993,
Modern Drummer

Calfskin Heads: Their History and Manufacture
by Gary Cook
Encyclopedia of Percussion

Skin Head Sources

Austrian Drumhead Company
Hans-Peter Kirbisser
+43 699 10 073 071
info@austriandrumheadcompany.at
www.austriandrumheadcompany.at

Bovid Percussion
Ryan McKay info@bovidpercussion.com
See pages XX of this book.
Bovid produces calf, goat, camel, and steer heads and mounts them on cold-rolled solid aluminum flesh hoops. Unique offerings include skins with hair and double-ply heads.

Vellum & Parchment Works Ltd.
21 Park Cres, Kimmage, Dublin, D12 Y79E, Ireland
Phone: +353 1 628 8270
This firm produces the famous "Velvet" white calf and "Kalfo" translucent skins. Skins are sold unmounted only, and payment is made by international wire transfer.

Altenburger Pergament und Trommelfell GmbH
Mozartstrasse 8, 04600 Altenburg
Germany
+ 49 3447 314010
www.pergament-trommelfell.de
info@pergament-trommelfell.de
Altenburger produces high-quality skins made from a number of different animals including calf, goat, and horse hides. Skins are sold unmounted only. In business since 1882.

WILLIAM COWLEY PARCHMENT MAKERS
Telephone - UK: 01908 610038
Worldwide: 0044 1908 610038
Email: enquiries@williamcowley.co.uk
Cowley sells unmounted skins only.

Parchment and Vellum Works
UK: 01908-610038
Fax 01908-611071
Worldwide: 0044-1908-610038
Fax 0044-1908-611071
Email: enquiries@williamcowley.co.uk
https://www.williamcowley.co.uk
Producer of high-quality white calf skins, sold unmounted only. In business since 1870, now in their fourth generation.

EARTHTONE HEADS
Gold Tone Music Group
3656 S. Hopkins Ave.
Titusville, FL 32780
1-800-826-5482
contact@earthtonedrumheads.com
Calfskin heads crimped into metal flash hoops with proprietary mounting system.

Professional Percussion Products
Karl Dustman
P.O. Box 33252, Cleveland, Ohio 44133
Phone: 440-877-9674 Fax: 440-877-9675
kbdustman@aol.com
www.professionalpercussionproducts.com/

Professional Drum Shop
854 Vine St, Los Angeles, CA 90038
(323) 469-6285 https://prodrumshop.com

Cooperman Company
1007 Route 121, Bellows Falls, VT 05101
coopermanvt@gmail.com www.cooperman.com
802 463 9750
Cooperman is a second-generation family business founded in 1961 by Patrick Cooperman. Cooperman specializes in rope tension drums, and drums, and a number of wood products. They produce (open, or unglued) wooden flesh hoops which are useful for making custom-sized drum heads.

STERN TANNING CO., INC.
contact info; see page 34
The last tannery to produce heads for the major American drum companies was the United Rawhide Company of Chicago, operated by Mr. Stephen Palansky. Palansky, a Czech immigrant, founded United Rawhide in 1951. As the American drum companies gave up their tanning operations in favor of mylar heads and purchasing finished skins, United Rawhide became the calfskin supplier to nearly all of the major players such as Gretsch, Ludwig, Slingerland, and Rogers. Eventually Mr. Palansky became the only American producer of heads for orchestral drums, outfits, and timpani.

When he retired, he sold his business to Stern Tanning and trained Stern in his manufacturing processes. Stern produces skins mounted on wooden flesh hoops as well as unmounted skins. They produce snare drum heads (white or translucent), bass drum heads, timpani heads, tambourine heads, bongo and conga heads, Taiko drum heads, and Bodhran drum heads.

Shipping Raw Skins For Tanning, from the Stern Tanning website:

STERN TANNING CO., INC.
4010 WEST DOUGLAS AVE.
MILWAUKEE, WI 53209

PHONE (414) 578-8615

E mail: info@sterntanning.com
www.sterntanning.com

HANDLING AND SHIPPING INSTRUCTIONS

AFTER SLAUGHTERING THE ANIMAL, ALLOW THE BLOOD TO RUN OFF AND THE PELT TO COOL DOWN. DO NOT USE WATER TO CLEAN THE SKIN. SCRAPE THE MEAT AND FAT CLEAN FROM THE SKIN, LAY THE PELT WOOL DOWN ON A FLAT SURFACE, AND IMMEDIATELY RUB 5 POUNDS OF FINE GRANULATED SALT INTO THE FLESH SIDE OF THE SKIN. IF USING PLYWOOD AS THE SURFACE, TILT PLYWOOD TO ALLOW DRAINAGE. STORE THE SKIN IN A DRY PLACE, OUT OF SUNLIGHT, AND ALLOW THE PELT TO SALT DRY UNTIL IT IS JUST PLIABLE. FOLD THE SKIN IN HALF, FLESH SIDE IN, REAR LEG TO REAR LEG AND FRONT LEG TO FRONT LEG. THE SKIN WILL THEN BE IN A CONDITION SUITABLE FOR SHIPPING.

FOR SHIPPING, PACK THE DRY SKIN IN A TIED UP PLASTIC BAG, AND SHIP IN A PAPER CARTON BOX TO THE ABOVE ADDRESS BY PARCEL POST OR OTHER PARCEL CARRIER. INCLUDE YOUR EMAIL, PHONE NUMBER, MAILING ADDRESS, AND RETURN SHIPPING ADDRESS INSIDE THE BOX.

WE CANNOT GUARANTEE AGAINST WOOL SLIPPAGE FROM THE SKIN. PROPER CARE OF THE SKIN IN THE RAW STAGE WILL HELP PREVENT WOOL SLIPPAGE.

IF THE SKIN HAS HOLES OR DEEP BUTCHER CUTS, THERE COULD BE A TOTAL OR PARTIAL LOSS OF THE SKIN IN THE PROCESS. WE WILL DO WHAT WE CAN TO WORK AROUND THE HOLES AND CUTS.

PRICES FOR HIDES RECEIVED AFTER 6/1/22 ARE AS FOLLOWS:

NUMBER OF LAMBSKIN TANNED	PRICE PER SKIN
1 – 4 HIDES	$68
5 OR MORE	$64

FOR LARGE HIDES WHERE FINISHED LENGTH (NECK TO TAIL) EXCEEDS 52", THERE WILL BE AN ADDITIONAL $6 CHARGE

A 50% DEPOSIT SHOULD BE INCLUDED WITH PELTS

PRICES DO NOT INCLUDE SHIPPING COSTS. AN INVOICE, INCLUDING SHIPPING CHARGES WILL BE SENT UPON COMPLETION OF TANNING. SKIN(S) WILL BE SHIPPED UPON RECEIPT OF PAYMENT OF THE BALANCE DUE.

PRICES SUBJECT TO CHANGE

ALL WORK DONE AT OWNERS RISK

Links to YouTube videos

Scotty Doucette demonstration of tucking calfskin onto wood flesh hoop: Recorded by Rob Cook at Jack's Drum Shop, Boston

https://www.youtube.com/watch?v=Px5-7-19KDQ

Rob Cook demonstration of tucking calfskin onto wood flesh hoop

https://youtu.be/fh98MnFtWUg

Rob Cook demonstration of laying up a wooden flesh hoop

https://www.youtube.com/watch?v=HIdwumN0hgM

REBEATS PUBLICATIONS
visit the Rebeats website or contact us for details

THE GRETSCH DRUM BOOK
by Rob Cook
with John Sheridan
Business history,
dating guide

THE SLINGERLAND BOOK
by Rob Cook
Business history,
dating guide

THE ROGERS BOOK
by Rob Cook
Business history,
dating guide

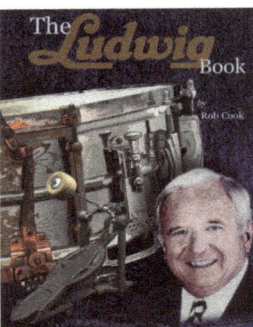
THE LUDWIG BOOK
by Rob Cook
Business history,
dating guide

THE MAKING OF A DRUM COMPANY
The autobiography of Wm. F. Ludwig II,
with Rob Cook

LEEDY DRUM TOPICS

THE LEEDY WAY
Biography of George Way,
History of Leedy, Camco,
Conn, L&S

MY LIFE IN PERCUSSION
Five Decades In The Music
Products Industry
Karl Dustman memoir

Franks For The Memories

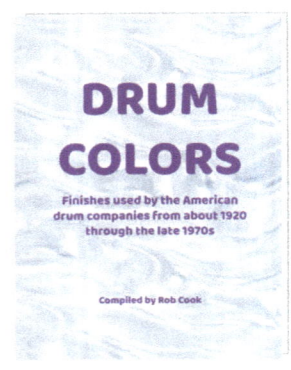
DRUM COLORS

George Way
mini-biography,
vendor directory

GENE KRUPA, HIS LIFE AND TIMES
biography of
Gene Krupa,
by Bruce Crowther

THE BABY DODDS STORY

Gretsch 1941
Catalog Reprint

HAL BLAINE & THE WRECKING CREW

Best Seat In The House

P.O. Box 6, Alma, Michigan 48801
989 463 4757
www.Rebeats.com   rob@rebeats.com